Barnacles Eat With Their Feet

Barnacles Eat With Their Feet

DELICIOUS FACTS ABOUT
THE TIDE POOL FOOD CHAIN

Text and Photographs by Sherry Shahan

THE MILLBROOK PRESS   BROOKFIELD, CONNECTICUT

Library of Congress Cataloging-in-Publication Data
Shahan, Sherry.
Barnacles eat with their feet : delicious facts about the tide pool food
chain / text and photographs by Sherry Shahan.
p. cm.
Summary: Describes the physical characteristics and eating habits of
plants, crustaceans, and other sea creatures that make their home in
tide pools.
ISBN 1-56294-922-5 (lib. bdg.)
1. Tide pool ecology—Juvenile literature. 2. Food chains (Ecology)—
Juvenile literature. [1. Tide pool ecology. 2. Food chains (Ecology). 3.
Ecology.] I. Title.
QH541.5.S35S48   1995
574.5′2638—dc20   95-21543   CIP   AC

Published by The Millbrook Press, Inc.
2 Old New Milford Road
Brookfield, CT 06804

For Michael Patrick

—Luv, Granola

WELCOME TO: TIDE POOLS
LOCATION: WORLDWIDE
POPULATION: UNKNOWN

Take a closer look . . .

Fill a glass to the rim with water. Now take a walk. Does the water spill? Probably.

Just as the water sloshes back and forth in the glass, the oceans slosh back and forth along coastlines. These movements are called **tides**. Tides are caused by the pull of the moon and the sun, which tug on the oceans with the force known as gravity.

Every day, there are two high tides, when water rises along the shore. And there are two low tides, when the water pulls away from the shore.

When the tide goes out, pools of water are left in rocky pockets along the shore. These water-filled pockets are tide pools. All around the world, countless sea plants and animals live in tide pools. And they all need food and nourishment.

High tide sets the table for the tide pool feast. Sea stars munch on mussels. Sea anemones nibble snails. Crabs dine on leftovers. But feeding time is short. When

the water withdraws, sea anemones pull in their **tentacles**. Barnacles and mussels snap shut, and crabs scurry under rocks.

That is, until the tide returns with another mouth-watering feast.

Plants

Most tide pool plants are seaweeds, members of the algae family. Unlike plants that grow on dry land, these plants don't have real roots, stems, and leaves. But tide pool seaweeds do have rootlike anchors called **holdfasts** that latch on to rocks. These anchors can stand up to waves with a force equal to winds of 125 miles (200 kilometers per hour). They can really hold fast!

An underwater forest of lush plant growth provides shelter for snails, worms, crabs, and lots of other creatures. Many animals munch on algae. So do you! A gelatinlike material called **agar** is made from certain types of algae. It is whipped into ice cream and cream cheese to make these foods smooth and silky.

Sea Urchin

The sea urchin is a spiny little creature with hundreds of tiny **tube feet**. The feet help it hold tight to tide pool rocks and reach its favorite food—seaweed.

The sea urchin's mouth is on the underside of its body. When it finds an algae-covered rock, it uses its sharp teeth to scrape the algae right off the rock. Sea urchins also use their sharp teeth to cut seaweed into tiny pieces. But it may take a sea urchin weeks to turn a clump of seaweed into a sea salad.

Abalone

A mild-mannered vegetarian, this abalone lives on the Pacific Coast. This ear-shaped **mollusk** creeps in the forests of seaweed that grow below the tide line. With its big foot clinging tightly to a rock, it can munch a bunch of seaweed, such as kelp and sea lettuce.

Barnacles

Barnacles cement themselves to tide pool rocks. They also hook on to mobile homes—buoys and boat bottoms. This **crustacean** spends its life upside down, using its fringed feet like silverware. Six pairs of feet sweep food particles from the water into the barnacle's body cavity.

Low tide leaves barnacles high and dry. Their shells squeeze shut until the tide returns—with a snack.

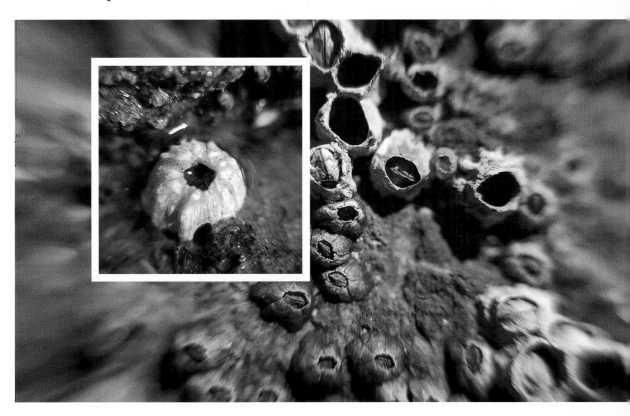

Clams and Mussels

Mussels attach themselves to rocks. Clams bury themselves in sand or mud. These stay-at-homes cannot go out to eat. Instead, they **filter feed**, drawing water over a network of gills. The gills are coated with mucus that snares microscopic side dishes, usually the **larvae** of other sea creatures and one-celled plants called **diatoms**. One large mussel can filter 1 1/5 quarts (1.5 liters) of water an hour and may devour 100,000 tidbits a day.

Snail

This amazing grazer has a special tongue called a **radula**. It is a hard, narrow ribbonlike structure armed with rows of chainsaw teeth that scrape algae off rocks. The radula also acts as a conveyor belt, carrying food to the stomach.

In this mollusk-eat-mollusk world, some snails have an appetite for their own kind. A snail is capable of boring a hole in another snail's shell and removing a take-out meal.

Chiton

Protected by a hard shell with mottled markings on its back, the rough-girdled chiton looks just like a splotch on the rock. But sometimes it isn't as harmless as it seems. The chiton raises one end of its mantle and waits for a worm to pass under. Snap! The trap springs shut, and the chiton dines. However, many members of the chiton family graze on algae.

Limpet

At night this gastropod, or "stomach foot," lifts its shell and stretches its foot. The slow-moving animal cruises during low tide in search of food to scrape off rocks. Some types of limpets burrow into sponges, munching them into new shapes. Others browse on red coralline algae.

Tube-Building Worm

Some worms build their houses with fine grains of sand, cemented together with sticky mucus. A group of these sand houses looks like a honeycomb. At high tide the worms use their tentacles to trap microscopic plants and animals, called **plankton**, that float in the sea soup.

Sea Cucumber

What's plump, thick-skinned, and a bit bumpy and warty? Did you answer "cucumber?" That's right—a sea cucumber.

This sluglike animal uses its tentacles to shovel bits of decaying matter and tiny plants and animals into its mouth. Some kinds of sea cucumbers cover themselves with poisonous mucus, so **predators** won't take a bite out of them.

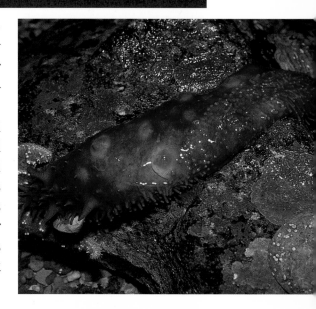

Tunicate

A tunicate, or sea squirt, draws water into its mouth over a large gill basket. As the water swirls in, small food particles stick to sheets of mucus. The food-laden mucus is then rolled into a spaghetti-like rope and passed to the stomach.

17

Sea Slug

The sea slug is called a nudibranch, a name that means "naked gills." This mollusk got that name because it has no shell. The sea-slug menu varies, since almost every sea-slug family has its favorite foods. Among them are sponges, fish eggs, and sea anemones. Sometimes sea slugs take on the color of the creature featured in their diet.

Sea Star

The sea star is a meat eater. It feeds on sand dollars, sea urchins, crabs, mussels, and other shellfish. But it has no teeth. How does it get its dinner?

This sea star attacks a shellfish by wrapping its arms around the shell in a game of tug-of-war. As soon as there's a hairline crack in the shell, the sea star will push its stomach through the opening. A belly full of jelly mixed with gastric juices digests the sea star's meal while it's still in the shell.

Brittle Star

This cousin of the sea star has a mouth shaped like a five-pointed star. Most brittle stars are suspension feeders. That is, they catch bits of plant and animal matter floating in the water. Sometimes they sweep their arms through the water, to catch as much as they can. Some **species** use their long tube feet to snare bristle worms and other small creatures, passing these tidbits from foot to mouth.

Sea Anemone

Do you see a flower sprouting on the back of a crab? Take a closer look. It may be a sea anemone. Most of the time, though, anemones hang out on rocks.

The anemone's petal-like tentacles have tiny stingers. The stingers paralyze small animals—crabs, shrimp, snails, and other meaty morsels—that blunder into the tentacles. Then the anemone pulls its **prey** toward its mouth, found in the center of its body. Anemones have been seen swallowing whole shore crabs, later spitting out bits of crab shell.

Rock Crab

Some tide pool animals aren't fussy when it comes to food. With pincers up and snapping, the rock crab goes after seaweed, worms, limpets, snails, and clams. More than once this decapod, or ten-legged animal, has mistaken a human toe for a tasty morsel. Ouch! Rock crabs also clean up the tide pool by eating dead plant and animal matter.

Sometimes a crab snatches a piece of sponge and plants it on its back. Weird table manners? Not really. The sponge is a clever disguise that fools hungry predators, like the octopus.

Hermit Crab

With six pairs of mouthparts, the hermit crab will eat just about any animal matter, dead or alive. It sometimes nibbles the tube feet of living sea urchins.

Prickleback Fish

A prickleback is a small eel-like fish that hangs out in shallow water. It's a **scavenger**, so it snacks on a variety of groceries, including larvae, worms, and shrimp.

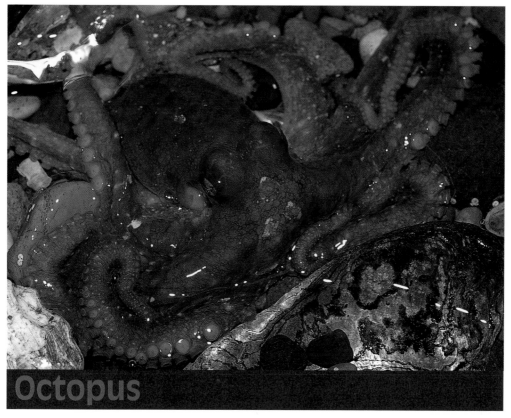

Octopus

Octopuses lurk in crevices among the rocks. Remember, it's OK to look—but don't touch. Some kinds of octopuses have a bite that is poisonous to people.

The octopus uses its parrotlike beak to break the shell of its favorite meal, crab. It injects a poison into its prey before returning to its den for a feast of cracked crab. Fish also rate high on the octopus menu.

Did you know that the suckers on this creature's eight arms can taste the difference between sweet and sour morsels?

Gull

No one has ever accused a gull of eating like a bird. Everything is fair game for this scavenger, which hangs out at tide pools—and at beaches, where it snatches scraps from picnickers. It's not unusual to see a gull grab a sandwich and swallow it whole. But when people aren't around, the gull favors a diet of crabs, snails, fish, and even sea stars.

Handle With Care

It's a good idea to wear an old pair of rain boots when you visit a tide pool. If you go barefoot, you may cut your feet on sharp rocks. If you wear shoes without boots, they'll get as wet as a water-soaked sponge. Remember to walk carefully on rocks so that barnacles, snails, and other small creatures won't be harmed.

Pick a rock and sit for a while. You will be amazed at the number of plants and animals calling one small area home. It's OK to move small rocks for a closer look. Just don't forget to put them back where you found them. Otherwise, lots of tiny creatures may end up with a bad case of heatstroke from too much sun, or be thrashed by pounding waves. Some may even be spotted by hungry predators.

Glossary

Crustacean—An animal with a hard outer shell, jointed limbs, and gills. Lobsters, crabs, and shrimps are all crustaceans.

Diatoms—Tiny one-celled plants in the algae family.

Filter feed—To get food by drawing water into the body and sifting food from it.

Holdfasts—The rootlike part of certain seaweeds that attaches the plant to a rock or other foundation.

Larvae—The early stage of an animal that changes in form when it becomes an adult. For example, a tadpole is the larva of a frog.

Mollusk—An animal with no backbone and a soft body, usually protected by a hard calcium shell. Snails, oysters, and clams are all mollusks.

Plankton—tiny plants and animals that drift with the ocean currents.

Predators—Animals that feed by hunting and killing other animals.

Prey—Animals that are hunted or killed for food.

Radula—A flexible, ribbonlike tongue with rows of sharp teeth, used for scraping food off surfaces.

Scavenger—An animal that eats waste matter.

Species—A single type of plant or animal that shares certain characteristics with others of its kind.

Tentacles—Long, flexible growths around the head or mouth of certain animals, used to feel, cling, grasp food, or move around.

Tide—the alternate rise and fall of the surface level of oceans.

Tube feet—Hollow, fluid-filled growths used by certain underwater animals for feeding and moving around. Sea stars and sea urchins have tube feet.

Index

About the Author

Author and photographer Sherry Shahan's assignments have taken her on horseback into Africa's Maasailand, hiking a leech-infested rain forest in Australia, and paddling a kayak in Alaska. And those are just the A's.

Her travel articles and photographs have appeared in dozens of international, national, and regional publications. She is also the author of several books for young readers. *Barnacles Eat With Their Feet* is her first book for The Millbrook Press.

When not out on an exciting assignment, she visits tide pools near her home on California's central coast.